The Entrepreneur's Book of Inspiration

MICHAEL ELLIOTT

The Entrepreneur's Book of Inspiration

The Go-to Manual for Entrepreneurs

OTHER BOOKS BY PEN & MANE PUBLISHING HOUSE

The Leader's Book of
Inspiration by Michael Elliott

Bulfinch's Mythology by
Thomas Bulfinch

*Go forth and spread your light,
putting pen to paper, spurring
souls to flight.*

Pen & Mane Publishing House

*Dedicated to God, to Whom all
things are owed.*

CONTENTS

INTRODUCTION

BY MICHAEL ELLIOTT

One can never be sure of the outcome of a new enterprise.

Bringing an idea to life can be exciting, yet, nerve-racking. Will it work? Is the idea good enough? Will people follow the vision?

We must tip our hats to entrepreneurs, for they ask these questions and hundreds more before embarking on the journey of starting a business. They rise above the often debilitating unknown, acting mainly on faith to get them to their desired destinations.

Economically invaluable to their countries, entrepreneurs chart their own course, preferring to hold their destinies in their own hands, rather than leave them to the whims of others.

They push the limits. They innovate. They create opportunities.

They dare.

They are the dreamers who brought this book to life.

How to Use this Book

This book is to be used as an invaluable companion to current and future entrepreneurs. Within these pages, you will read insights from CEOs, entrepreneurs and business visionaries, as well as other extraordinary minds.

Each chapter represents a stone along the entrepreneurial path.

The book begins with "Dreams" and ends with "Happiness," may your entrepreneurial journey do the same.

I
Look to the Stars:
Book of Dreams

"Whatever you can do, or dream you can, begin it. Boldness has genius, power and magic in it."

W. H. Murray

The future belongs to those who believe
in the beauty of their dreams.
-Eleanor Roosevelt

Laughter is timeless. Imagination has no
age. And dreams are forever.
-Walt Disney

The size of your success is measured by
the strength of your desire; the size of
your dream; and how you handle
disappointment along the way.
-Robert Kiyosaki

The dreamers of the day are dangerous…
for they may act their dream with open
eyes, to make it possible.
-T.E. Lawrence

Man, alone, has the power to transform
his thoughts into physical reality; man,
alone, can dream and make his dreams
come true.
-Napoleon Hill

It is not in the stars to hold our destiny
but in ourselves.
-William Shakespeare

It's difficult to follow your dream. It's a tragedy not to.
-*Ralph Marston*

No one has ever achieved anything from the smallest to the greatest unless the dream was dreamed first.
-*Laura Ingalls Wilder*

Too many of us are not living our dreams because we are living our fears.
-*Les Brown*

Dream big. Start small. But most of all,
start.
-Simon Sinek

Most men lead lives of quiet desperation
and go to the grave with the song still in
them.
-Henry David Thoreau

As you move toward a dream, the dream
moves toward you.
- Julia Cameron.

On your journey to your dream, be ready
to face oasis and deserts. In both cases,
don't stop
-Paulo Coelho

When you have a dream, you've got to
grab it and never let go.
-Carol Burnett

Hold fast to dreams, for if dreams die, life
is a broken-winged bird that cannot fly.
-Langston Hughes

All your dreams can come true if you
have the courage to pursue them.
-Walt Disney

A dream is a microscope through which
we look at the hidden occurrences in our
soul.
-Erich Fromm

What would you dare to dream if you
knew you wouldn't fail?
-Brian Tracy

Dreams are the touchstones of our
character.
-Henry David Thoreau

If you follow your dreams and spend
your life doing what brings you joy, you
are more likely to find success
-Richard Branson

Dreams are the touchstones of our
character.
There is only one thing that makes a
dream impossible to achieve: the fear of
failure.
-Paulo Coelho

Your dream has to be bigger than your
fear.
-Steve Harvey

Don't be pushed by your problems. Be
led by your dreams.
-Ralph Waldo Emerson

You face the biggest challenge of all: to
have the courage to seek your big dream
regardless of what anyone says. You are
the only person alive who can see your
big picture and even you can't see it all.
-Oprah Winfrey

Never give up on a dream just because of the time it will take to accomplish it. The time will pass anyway.
-*Earl Nightingale*

Dreams require down payments. Dreams are free, but the journey isn't. There is a price to pay. When you find your why you'll find your way. When you develop your will you will embark on your way. Many people start; few people finish. Many people have a dream; few people achieve their dreams.
-*John C. Maxwell*

II
Refiner's Fire:
Book of Discipline

"Self-respect is the fruit of discipline; the sense of dignity grows with the ability to say no to oneself."
Abraham Joshua Heschel

The discipline of desire is the background
of character.
-John Locke

One can have no smaller or greater
mastery than mastery of oneself.
-Leonardo da Vinci

Discipline is choosing between what you
want now, and what you want most.
-Abraham Lincoln

You can never conquer the mountain.
You can only conquer yourself.
-Jim Whittaker

He who requires much from himself and little from others, will keep himself from being the object of resentment.
- Confucius

If you do not conquer self, you will be conquered by self.
-Napoleon Hill

Discipline, work. Work, discipline.
-Gustav Mahler

You have power over your mind - not outside events. Realize this, and you will find strength.
-Marcus Aurelius

Genius is the capacity for receiving and improving by discipline.
-George Eliot

Men are anxious to improve their
circumstances, but are unwilling to
improve themselves; they therefore
remain bound.
-James Allen

He who reigns within himself and rules
passions, desires, and fears is more than a
king.
-John Milton

We all have dreams. But in order to make
dreams come into reality, it takes an
awful lot of determination, dedication,
self-discipline, and effort.
-Jesse Owens

Discipline is the difference between what you want now and what you want most.
-Unknown

Active valour may often be the present of nature; but such patient diligence can be the fruit only of habit and discipline.
-Edward Gibbon

Such power there is in clear-eyed self-restraint.
-James Russell Lowell

This quality of self-denial in pursuit of a
longer-term goal and, indeed, the
willpower to maintain the denial, is
excellent training for the boardroom.
-John Viney

Man must be disciplined, for he is by
nature raw and wild.
- Immanuel Kant

Industry, thrift and self-control are not
sought because they create wealth, but
because they create character.
-Calvin Coolidge

Success is nothing more than a few
simple disciplines, practiced every day.
-Jim Rohn

No man is free who is not master of
himself.
-Epictetus

.

Discipline is the soul of an army. It makes
small numbers formidable; procures
success to the weak, and esteem to all.
-George Washington

If we can look upon our work not for self-benefit, but as a means to benefit society, we will be practicing appreciation and patience in our daily lives.
-Gautama Buddha

Those who can command themselves command others.
-William Hazlitt

Emotions were like wild horses and it required wisdom to be able to control them
-Paulo Coelho

In reading the lives of great men, I found that the first victory they won was over themselves… self-discipline with all of them came first.
-Harry S. Truman

True genius, in strategy or anywhere, lies in self-control, self-mastery, presence of mind, fluidity of thought.
-Robert Greene

Disciplining yourself to do what you know is right and important, although difficult, is the highroad to pride, self-esteem, and personal satisfaction.
-Margaret Thatcher

III
The Doorway:
Book of Knowledge

"The noblest pleasure is the joy of understanding."
Leonardo da Vinci

Education is the ability to listen to almost
anything without losing your temper or
your self-confidence.
-Robert Frost

All I have learned, I learned from books.
-Abraham Lincoln

All men who have turned out worth
anything have had the chief hand in their
own education.
-Sir Walter Scott

Education breeds confidence. Confidence breeds hope. Hope breeds peace.
-Confucius

Risk comes from not knowing what you're doing
-Warren Buffett

A single conversation across the table with a wise man is better than ten years mere study of books.
-Henry Wadsworth Longfellow

Only the educated are free.
-Epictetus

A man will be imprisoned in a room with
a door that's unlocked and opens
inwards; as long as it does not occur to
him to pull rather than push.
-Ludwig Wittgenstein

The only real mistake is the one from
which we learn nothing.
-Henry Ford

It is the mark of an educated mind to be able to entertain a thought without accepting it.
-Aristotle

Curiosity is the wick in the candle of learning.
-William Arthur Ward

Formal education will make you a living; self-education will make you a fortune.
-Jim Rohn

Education is not the filling of a pail, but
the lighting of a fire.
-William Butler Yeats

Intelligence plus character-that is the goal
of true education.
-Martin Luther King Jr.

A University should be a place of light, of
liberty, and of learning
-Benjamin Disraeli

Education is a progressive discovery of
our own ignorance.
-Will Durant

Study without desire spoils the memory,
and it retains nothing that it takes in.
-Leonardo da Vinci

It does not matter how slowly you go as
long as you do not stop.
-Confucius

The job of an educator is to teach
students to see vitality in themselves
-Joseph Campbell

Wisdom…. comes not from age, but from
education and learning.
-Anton Chekhov

What we become depends on what we
read after all of the professors have
finished with us. The greatest university
of all is a collection of books.
-Thomas Carlyle

The world is a book and those who do
not travel read only one page.
-St. Augustine

Ignorance is the parent of fear.
-Herman Melville

Learning is not compulsory; it's
voluntary… But to survive, we must
learn.
-W. Edwards Deming

Self-education is, I firmly believe, the
only kind of education there is.
-Isaac Asimov

The task of the modern educator is not to
cut down jungles, but to irrigate deserts.
-C.S. Lewis

Teaching is not a lost art, but the regard
for it is a lost tradition.
-Jacques Barzun

By seeking and blundering we learn.
-Johann Wolfgang von Goethe

Educating the mind without educating
the heart is no education at all.
-Aristotle

Education is our passport to the future,
for tomorrow belongs to the people who
prepare for it today.
-Malcolm X

Whatever the cost of our libraries, the price is cheap compared to that of an ignorant nation.
-Walter Cronkite

All of life is a constant education.
-Eleanor Roosevelt

To make no mistakes is not in the power of man; but from their errors and mistakes the wise and good learn wisdom for the future.
-Plutarch

I think the big mistake in schools is trying to teach children anything, and by using fear as the basic motivation. Fear of getting failing grades, fear of not staying with your class, etc. Interest can produce learning on a scale compared to fear as a nuclear explosion to a firecracker.
-Stanley Kubrick

IV
Sapphire Tapestry: Book of Creativity

"An essential aspect of creativity is not being afraid to fail."

Edwin Land

Any activity becomes creative when the
doer cares about doing it right or better.
-John Updike

Great ideas often receive violent
opposition from mediocre minds.
-Albert Einstein

I am seeking, I am striving, I am in it with
all my heart.
-Vincent Van Gogh

When you ask creative people how they did something, they feel a little guilty because they didn't really do it, they just saw something.
-Steve Jobs

This world is but a canvas to our imagination.
-Henry David Thoreau

Create. Not for the money. Not for the fame. Not for the recognition. But for the pure joy of creating something and sharing it.
-Ernest Barbaric

The visionary starts with a clean sheet of
paper, and re-imagines the world.
-Malcolm Gladwell

Most people die before they are fully
born. Creativeness means to be born
before one dies.
-Erich Fromm

Some painters transform the sun into a
yellow spot, others transform a yellow
spot into the sun.
-Pablo Picasso

Creative work is play. It is free
speculation using materials of ones
chosen form.
-Stephen Nachmanovitch

The best way to predict the future is to
create it.
-Peter Drucker

A creative man is motivated by the desire
to achieve, not by the desire to beat
others.
-Ayn Rand

A business has to be involving, it has to
be fun, and it has to exercise your
creative instincts.
-Richard Branson

You have to create something from
nothing.
-Ralph Lauren

Openly share and talk to people about
your idea. Use their lack of interest or
doubt to fuel your motivation to make it
happen.
-Todd Garland

Creativity is always a leap of faith. You're faced with a blank page, blank easel, or an empty stage.
-Julia Cameron

There's no shortage of remarkable ideas, what's missing is the will to execute them.
-Seth Godin

It's not what you look at that matters, it's what you see.
-Henry David Thoreau

Creativity takes courage.
-*Henri Matisse*

Every human has four endowments - self awareness, conscience, independent will and creative imagination. These give us the ultimate human freedom… The power to choose, to respond, to change.
-*Stephen Covey*

At first they'll ask you why you're doing it. Later they'll ask how you did it.
-*Unknown*

In the modern world of business, it is useless to be a creative, original thinker unless you can also sell what you create.
-David Ogilvy

In the creative state a man is taken out of himself. He lets down as it were a bucket into his subconscious, and draws up something which is normally beyond his reach. He mixes this thing with his normal experiences and out of the mixture he makes a work of art.
-E. M. Forster

The monotony and solitude of a quiet life
stimulates the creative mind.
-Albert Einstein

I'm always thinking about creating. My
future starts when I wake up every
morning… Every day I find something
creative to do with my life.
-Miles Davis

Genius… means little more than the
faculty of perceiving in an unhabitual
way.
-William James

V
Light the Way:
Book of Motivation

"View your life from your funeral: Looking back at your life experiences, what have you accomplished? What would you have wanted to accomplish but didn't? What were the happy moments? What were the sad? What would you do again, and what wouldn't you do?"

Victor Frankl

In the end, a vision without the ability to execute it is probably a hallucination.
-Steve Case

Behold the turtle. It makes progress only when it sticks its neck out.
-James Bryant

Every problem is a gift — without problems we would not grow.
-Tony Robbins

Being defeated is often a temporary condition. Giving up is what makes it permanent.
-Marilyn vos Savant

Act enthusiastic and you will be enthusiastic.
-Dale Carnegie

Fearlessness is like a muscle. I know from my own life that the more I exercise it the more natural it becomes to not let my fears run me.
-Arianna Huffington

When something is important enough,
you do it even if the odds are not in your
favor.
-Elon Musk

It is not what they take away from you
that counts. It's what you do with what
you have left.
-Hubert H. Humphrey

The man on top of the mountain didn't
fall there.
-Vince Lombardi

If you are going through hell, keep going.
-Winston Churchill

Don't let others define you. Don't let the past confine you. Take charge of your life with confidence and determination and there are no limits on what you can do or be.
-Michael Josephson

The man who moves a mountain begins by carrying away small stones.
-Confucius

Great minds discuss ideas; average
minds discuss events; small minds
discuss people.
-Eleanor Roosevelt

If not you, who? If not now, when?
-Hillel the Elder

If you worry about yesterday's failures,
then today's successes will be few. The
future depends on what we do in the
present.
-Mahatma Gandhi

Everyone thinks of changing the world,
but no one thinks of changing himself.
-Leo Tolstoy

Someone once told me growth and
comfort do not coexist. and I think it's a
really good thing to remember.
-Ginni Rometty

Vision without action is a daydream.
Action without vision is a nightmare
–Japanese Proverb

Don't limit yourself. Many people limit themselves to what they think they can do. You can go as far as your mind lets you. What you believe, remember, you can achieve.
-Mary Kay Ash

You don't learn to walk by following rules. You learn by doing and falling over.
-Richard Branson

Ninety-nine percent of the failures come from people who have the habit of making excuses.
-George Washington Carver

Don't say you don't have enough time.
You have exactly the same number of
hours per day that were given to Helen
Keller, Pasteur, Michelangelo, Mother
Teresa, Leonardo Da Vinci, Thomas
Jefferson, and Albert Einstein.
-H. Jackson Brown

Don't wait for opportunity. Create it.
-Unknown

You never know how strong you are,
until being strong is your only choice.
-Bob Marley

High expectations are the key to
everything.
-Sam Walton

If you hear a voice within you say 'you
cannot paint,' then by all means paint,
and that voice will be silenced.
-Vincent Van Gogh

Risk more than others think is safe.
Dream more than others think is
practical.
-Howard Schultz

Stop chasing the money and start chasing
the passion.
-Tony Hsieh

Embrace what you don't know,
especially in the beginning, because what
you don't know can become your
greatest asset. It ensures that you will
absolutely be doing things different from
everybody else.
-Sara Blakely

The way to get started is to quit talking
and begin doing.
-Walt Disney

People often say that motivation doesn't last. Well, neither does bathing – that's why we recommend it daily.
-*Zig Ziglar*

Start by doing what's necessary; then do what's possible; and suddenly you are doing the impossible.
-*Francis of Assisi*

Everything is hard before it is easy.
Johann Wolfgang von Goethe

My biggest motivation? Just to keep challenging myself. I see life almost like one long University education that I never had — every day I'm learning something new.
-Richard Branson

If you want to be respected, you must respect yourself.
-Spanish Proverb

Do more than belong: participate. Do more than care: help. Do more than believe: practice. Do more than be fair: be kind. Do more than forgive: forget. Do more than dream: work.
-William Arthur Ward

Stop waiting for others to tell you what you can do. Start putting faith into your own strengths and talents. Instead of questioning whether you can reach your goals, move forward with conviction and confidence.
-Jane Powell

No matter how many mistakes you make or how slow you progress, you are still way ahead of everyone who isn't trying.
-Tony Robbins

Somebody should tell us, right at the start of our lives, that we are dying. Then we might live life to the limit, every minute of every day. Do it! I say. Whatever you want to do, do it now! There are only so many tomorrows.
-*Pope Paul VI*

There are lots of bad reasons to start a company. But there's only one good, legitimate reason, and I think you know what it is: it's to change the world.
-Phil Libin

It's not about ideas. It's about making ideas happen.
-Scott Belsky

Your time is limited, so don't waste it living someone else's life. Don't be trapped by dogma – which is living with the results of other people's thinking. Don't let the noise of other's opinions drown out your own inner voice. And most importantly, have the courage to follow your heart and intuition. They somehow already know what you truly want to become. Everything else is secondary.
-*Steve Jobs*

VI
Eagle's Wings:
Book of Marble

*"Life's most persistent and urgent question
is, 'What are you doing for others?"*
Martin Luther King Jr.

The growth and development of people
is the highest calling of leadership.
-Harvey S. Firestone

Alone we can do so little; together we can
do so much.
-Helen Keller

If you do not look at things on a large
scale, it will be difficult to master
strategy.
-Miyamoto Musashi

In matters of style, swim with the
current; in matters of principle, stand like
a rock.
-Thomas Jefferson

The final test of a leader is that he leaves
behind him in other men the conviction
and the will to carry on.
-Walter Lippmann

Leadership is a matter of having people
look at you and gain confidence, seeing
how you react. If you're in control,
they're in control.
-Tom Landry

Outstanding leaders go out of their way
to boost the self-esteem of their
personnel. If people believe in
themselves, it's amazing what they can
accomplish.
-Sam Walton

A leader is one who knows the way, goes
the way, and shows the way.
-John C. Maxwell

Become the kind of leader that people
would follow voluntarily; even if you
had no title or position.
-Brian Tracy

Good leaders must first become good
servants.
-Robert K. Greenleaf

When I give a minister an order, I leave it
to him to find the means to carry it out.
-Napoleon Bonaparte

Leadership is based on a spiritual quality;
the power to inspire, the power to inspire
others to follow
-Vince Lombardi

The secret of leadership is simple: Do what you believe in. Paint a picture of the future. Go there. People will follow.
-Seth Godin

Good business leaders create a vision, articulate the vision, passionately own the vision, and relentlessly drive it to completion.
-Jack Welch

The greatness of a leader is measured by the achievements of the led. This is the ultimate test of his effectiveness.
-Omar N. Bradley

The man of genius inspires us with a
boundless confidence in our own powers.
-Ralph Waldo Emerson

Kind words can be short and easy to
speak, but their echoes are truly endless.
-Mother Teresa

The task of leadership is not to put
greatness into people, but to elicit it, for
the greatness is there already.
-John Buchan

A leader is best when people barely
know he exists, when his work is done,
his aim fulfilled, they will say: we did it
ourselves.
-Lao Tzu

Leadership is no longer about your
position.
It's now more about your passion for
excellence and making a difference.
You can lead without a title.
-Robin Sharma

No man will make a great leader who
wants to do it all himself, or to get all the
credit for doing it.
-Andrew Carnegie

The best executive is one who has sense enough to pick good people to do what he wants done, and self-restraint enough to keep from meddling with them while they do it.
-Theodore Roosevelt

A leader must have the courage to act against an expert's advice.
-James Callaghan

Leadership is a potent combination of strategy and character. But if you must be without one, be without the strategy.
-Norman Schwarzkopf

Leadership is about making others better
as a result of your presence and making
sure that impact lasts in your absence.
-Sheryl Sandberg

Don't find fault, find a remedy.
-Henry Ford

The greatest leader is not necessarily the
one who does the greatest things. He is
the one that gets the people to do the
greatest things.
-Ronald Reagan

To give real service you must add
something which cannot be bought or
measured with money, and that is
sincerity and integrity.
-Douglas Adams

Leadership is the capacity to translate
vision into reality.
-Warren G. Bennis

Leaders don't complain about what's not
working. Leaders celebrate what is
working and work to amplify it.
-Simon Sinek

The world is starving for original and
decisive leadership.
-Bryant H. McGill

Before you become a leader, success is all
about growing yourself. After you
become a leader, success is about
growing others.
-Jack Welch

Management is efficiency in climbing the
ladder of success; leadership determines
whether the ladder is leaning against the
right wall.
-Stephen Covey

If you set out to be liked, you would be prepared to compromise on anything at any time, and you would achieve nothing.
-*Margaret Thatcher*

Leaders don't create followers, they create more leaders.
-*Tom Peters*

The leader sees leadership as responsibility rather than as rank and privilege.
-*Peter Drucker*

Innovation distinguishes between a
leader and a follower.
-Steve Jobs

There's only one way to succeed in
anything, and that is to give it
everything.
-Vince Lombardi

The man who promises everything is
sure to fulfill nothing, and everyone who
promises too much is in danger of using
evil means in order to carry out his
promises, and is already on the road to
perdition.
-Carl Jung

Keep away from people who try to belittle your ambitions. Small people always do that, but the really great make you feel that you, too, can become great.
-Mark Twain

Every person has a longing to be significant; to make a contribution; to be a part of something noble and purposeful.
-John C. Maxwell

To govern was to serve, not to rule.
-Seneca the Younger

Make your team feel respected,
empowered and genuinely excited about
the company's mission.
-Tim Westergen

If your actions inspire others to dream
more, learn more, do more and become
more, you are a leader.
-John Quincy Adams

It's never crowded along the extra mile.
-Wayne Dyer

Leaders think and talk about the
solutions. Followers think and talk about
the problems.
-Brian Tracy

Nothing so conclusively proves a man's
ability to lead others as what he does
from day to day to lead himself.
-Thomas J. Watson

Storytelling is the most powerful way to
put ideas into the world today.
-Robert McKee

The mind is not a vessel to be filled but a
fire to be kindled.
-Plutarch

Leadership is hard to define and good
leadership even harder. But if you can get
people to follow you to the ends of the
earth, you are a great leader.
-Indra Nooyi

The leader is the person who brings a
little magic to the moment.
-Denise Morrison

A leader is a dealer in hope.
-*Napoleon Bonaparte*

Leaders, whether in the family, in business, in government, or in education, must not allow themselves to mistake intentions for accomplishments.
-*Jim Rohn*

A true leader has the confidence to stand alone, the courage to make tough decisions, and the compassion to listen to the needs of others. He does not set out to be a leader, but becomes one by the equality of his actions and the integrity of his intent.
-*Douglas MacArthur*

VII
Think with the Heart: Book of Giving

"If you wait until you can do everything for everybody, instead of something for somebody, you'll end up not doing nothing for nobody."

Malcolm Bane

No person was ever honored for what he received. Honor has been the reward for what he gave.
-Calvin Coolidge

The highest use of capital is not to make more money, but to make money do more for the betterment of life.
-Henry Ford

Give what you have. To some one, it may be better than you dare to think.
-Henry Wadsworth Longfellow

No one is useless in this world who
lightens the burden of it to anyone else.
-Charles Dickens

Act as if what you do makes a difference.
It does.
-William James

Generosity is giving more than you can,
and pride is taking less than you need.
-Khalil Gibran

The true meaning of life is to plant trees,
under whose shade you do not expect to
sit.
-Nelson Henderson

The best way to find yourself is to lose
yourself in the service of others.
-Mahatma Gandhi

To ease another's heartache is to forget
one's own.
-Abraham Lincoln

When we give cheerfully and accept
gratefully, everyone is blessed.
-Maya Angelou

Happiness is not so much in having as
sharing. We make a living by what we
get, but we make a life by what we give.
-Norman MacEwen

Real generosity toward the future lies in
giving all to the present.
-Albert Camus

Wealth is not to feed our egos but to feed
the hungry and to help people help
themselves.
-Andrew Carnegie

Real generosity is doing something nice
for someone who will never find out.
-Frank A. Clark

The life of a man consists not in seeing
visions and in dreaming dreams, but in
active charity and in willing service.
-Henry Wadsworth Longfellow

True charity is the desire to be useful to others with no thought of recompense.
-*Emanuel Swedenborg*

To give without any reward, or any notice, has a special quality of its own.
-*Anne Morrow Lindbergh*

You give but little when you give of your possessions. It is when you give of yourself that you truly give.
-*Khalil Gibran*

Let us not be satisfied with just giving money. Money is not enough, money can be got, but they need your hearts to love them. So, spread your love everywhere you go.
-*Mother Teresa*

VIII
Journey of a Thousand Miles:
Book of Success

The real secret of success is enthusiasm.
-Walter Chrysler

There is never a bad time to start a business – unless you want to start a mediocre one.
-Gary Vaynerchuk

Success is not a function of the size of your title but the richness of your contribution.
-Robin Sharma

The most successful people in life are the ones who ask questions. They're always learning. They're always growing. They're always pushing.
-Robert Kiyosaki

If you don't find a way to make money while you sleep, you will work until you die.
-Warren Buffet

Each day that you're moving toward your dreams without compromising who you are, you're winning.
-Michael Dell

If you decide that you're going to do only
the things you know are going to work,
you're going to leave a lot of opportunity
on the table.
-Jeff Bezos

Success is knowing your purpose in life,
growing to reach your maximum
potential, and sowing seeds that benefit
others.
-John C. Maxwell

Concentrate your energies, your thoughts
and your capital. The wise man puts all
his eggs in one basket and watches the
basket.
-Andrew Carnegie

Decide that you are not going to stay
where you are.
-J. P. Morgan

All successful people men and women
are big dreamers. They imagine what
their future could be, ideal in every
respect, and then they work every day
toward their distant vision, that goal or
purpose.
-Brian Tracy

The entrepreneur always searches for
change, responds to it, and exploits it as
an opportunity.
-Peter Drucker

Many of life's failures are people who did
not realize how close they were to
success when they gave up.
-*Thomas A. Edison*

The biggest risk is not taking any risk…
In a world that is changing really quickly,
the only strategy that is guaranteed to fail
is not taking risks.
-*Mark Zuckerberg*

The secret of my success is a two word
answer: Know people.
-*Harvey S. Firestone*

The foundation stones for a balanced
success are honesty, character, integrity,
faith, love and loyalty.
-*Zig Ziglar*

Success does not consist in never making
mistakes but in never making the same
one a second time.
-*George Bernard Shaw*

Around here, however, we don't look backward for very long. We keep moving forward, opening new doors, and doing new things, because we're curious and curiosity keeps leading us down new paths.
-*Walt Disney*

I do not think that there is any other quality so essential to success of any kind as the quality of perseverance. It overcomes almost everything, even nature.
-John D. Rockefeller

I'm convinced that about half of what separates the successful entrepreneurs from the non-successful ones is pure perseverance.
-Steve Jobs

The path to success is to take massive, determined action.
-Tony Robbins

Success is a lousy teacher. It seduces
smart people into thinking they can't
lose.
-Bill Gates

Don't mistake activity with achievement.
-John Wooden

Success comes to those who have an
entire mountain of gold that they
continually mine, not those who find one
nugget and try to live on it for fifty years.
-John C. Maxwell

It's better to hang out with people better
than you. Pick out associates whose
behavior is better than yours and you'll
drift in that direction.
-Warren Buffet

It is better to fail in originality than to
succeed in imitation.
-Herman Melville

Celebrate your successes. Find some
humor in your failures.
-Sam Walton

To succeed, jump as quickly at
opportunities as you do at conclusions.
-Benjamin Franklin

The size of your success is measured by
the strength of your desire; The size of
your dream; And how you handle
disappointment along the way.
-Robert Kiyosaki

Success is empty if you arrive at the
finish line alone.
-Howard Schultz

Successful people are always looking for
opportunities to help others.
Unsuccessful people are always asking,
'What's in it for me?'
-Brian Tracy

Plans are only good intentions unless
they immediately degenerate into hard
work.
-Peter Drucker

Success is neither magical nor
mysterious. Success is the natural
consequence of consistently applying the
basic fundamentals.
-Jim Rohn

Only those who dare to fail greatly can
ever achieve greatly.
-Robert F. Kennedy

Move fast and break things. Unless you
are breaking stuff, you are not moving
fast enough.
-Mark Zuckerberg

The secret of success is learning how to
use pain and pleasure instead of having
pain and pleasure use you. If you do that,
you're in control of your life. If you don't,
life controls you.
-Tony Robbins

Before everything else, getting ready is
the secret of success.
-Henry Ford

Achievement happens when we pursue
and attain what we want. Success comes
when we are in clear pursuit of why we
want it.
-Simon Sinek

Try never to be the smartest person in the
room. And if you are, I suggest you invite
smarter people or find a different room.
-Michael Dell

There is little success where there is little
laughter.
-Andrew Carnegie

You have to be willing to be
misunderstood if you're going to
innovate.
-Jeff Bezos

I'm a success today because I had a friend
who believed in me and I didn't have the
heart to let him down.
-Abraham Lincoln

Success unshared is failure.
-John Paul DeJoria

Fun is one of the most important - and
underrated - ingredients in any
successful venture. If you're not having
fun, then it's probably time to call it quits
and try something else.
-Richard Branson

If you want to succeed you should strike
out on new paths, rather than travel the
worn paths of accepted success.
-John D. Rockefeller

Being aware of your fear is smart.
Overcoming it is the mark of a successful
person.
-Seth Godin

When one side benefits more than the
other, that's a win-lose situation. To the
winner it might look like success for a
while, but in the long run, it breeds
resentment and distrust.
-Stephen Covey

The secret of your success is determined
by your daily agenda.
-John C. Maxwell

Never was anything great achieved
without danger.
-Niccolo Machiavelli

It's fine to celebrate success but it is more
important to heed the lessons of failure.
-Bill Gates

Whatever the mind can conceive and
believe, it can achieve.
-Napoleon Hill

Success is the sum of details.
-Harvey S. Firestone

Rich people have small TVs and big libraries, and poor people have small libraries and big TVs.
-Zig Ziglar

Go as far as you can see; when you get there you'll be able to see farther.
-J. P. Morgan

Your work is going to fill a large part of your life, and the only way to be truly satisfied is to do what you believe is great work. And the only way to do great work is to love what you do. If you haven't found it yet, keep looking. Don't settle. As with all matters of the heart, you'll know when you find it.
-Steve Jobs

It is hard to fail, but it is worse never to have tried to succeed.
-Theodore Roosevelt

All our dreams can come true, if we have the courage to pursue them.
-Walt Disney

IX
May Your Cup Runneth Over: Book of Happiness

> *"The foolish man seeks happiness in the distance, the wise grows it under his feet."*
> James Oppenheim

Now and then it's good to pause in our
pursuit of happiness and just be happy.
-Guillaume Apollinaire

Happiness depends upon ourselves.
-Aristotle

The greatest happiness comes from being
vitally interested in something that
excites all your energies.
-Walter Annenberg

The person born with a talent they are meant to use will find their greatest happiness in using it.
-*Johann Wolfgang von Goethe*

Happiness is when what you think, what you say, and what you do are in harmony.
-*Mahatma Gandhi*

All happiness depends on courage and work.
-*Honoré de Balzac*

If more of us valued food and cheer and
song above hoarded gold, it would be a
merrier world.
-J.R.R. Tolkien

Man only likes to count his troubles; he
doesn't calculate his happiness.
-Fyodor Dostoevsky

Happiness depends more on the inward
disposition of mind than on outward
circumstances.
-Benjamin Franklin

With all its sham, drudgery, and broken
dreams,
it is still a beautiful world.
Be cheerful.
Strive to be happy.
-Max Ehrmann

The happiness of your life depends upon
the quality of your thoughts.
-Marcus Aurelius

Until you are happy with who you are,
you will never be happy with what you
have.
-Zig Ziglar

Learn to value yourself, which means:
fight for your happiness.
-Ayn Rand

Let us be grateful to the people who
make us happy; they are the charming
gardeners who make our souls blossom.
-Marcel Proust

Let no one ever come to you without
leaving better and happier. Be the living
expression of God's kindness: kindness in
your face, kindness in your eyes,
kindness in your smile.
-Mother Teresa

Human happiness and moral duty are
inseparably connected.
-George Washington

Whoever is happy will make others
happy.
-Anne Frank

So we shall let the reader answer this
question for himself: who is the happier
man, he who has braved the storm of life
and lived or he who has stayed securely
on shore and merely existed?
-Hunter S. Thompson

About

MICHAEL ELLIOTT, a speaker and writer, is the President of Idea Zero, creator of The Michael Elliott Podcast and founder of Mind&Soul Society.

www.ideazero.co

www.michaelelliott.net

www.mindandsoulsociety.com

Index

C

D

E

I

J

Joseph Campbell, 28
Julia Cameron, 5, 41

K

Khalil Gibran, 83, 87

L

Langston Hughes, 6
Lao Tzu, 68
Laura Ingalls Wilder, 4
Leonardo da Vinci, 12, 21, 27
Leo Tolstoy, 51
Les Brown, 4
Ludwig Wittgenstein, 24

M

Mahatma Gandhi, 50, 84, 111
Malcolm Bane, 81
Malcolm Gladwell, 38
Malcolm X, 31

O

P

R

V

W

Z

Zig Ziglar, 56, 95, 107, 113

www.ingramcontent.com/pod-product-compliance
Lightning Source LLC
Chambersburg PA
CBHW022218050726
47590CB00002B/860